A FAMILY
is like a
Cake

To Samuel, Missy and Dan
— Shona Innes

For the best family that I have ever met:
Emma, Juli, Panna, Szonja, Bori, Ági and Ali
— Írisz Agócs

FIVE MILE

Five Mile, an imprint of
Bonnier Publishing Australia
Level 6, 534 Church Street,
Richmond, Victoria 3121
www.fivemile.com.au

First published 2017
Printed in China 5 4 3 2 1

A FAMILY
is like a
Cake

Shona Innes * Írisz Agócs

FIVE MILE

Our family are the people we feel we belong to.

Families are the people who think about us and
remember us and watch us as we grow and change.

Families are the people who help us feel we belong.

When we are with our family – wherever we might be in the world – we feel like we are home.

Families can help you feel you belong,
even when you are apart from them.

Families give us help, support and love.

Growing up in a family is a lot like making a fabulous cake. Cakes can be different shapes and sizes, flavours, colours and layers.

That's because cakes are made up of many different ingredients, which are then mixed together in careful ways and baked to create something truly delicious and amazing.

A family is a bit like a cake.

Families come in different shapes and different sizes.

Some are sweet and some can be a bit spicy.
Some have extra ingredients and some have just a few.

Some families are warm and gooey or cool and firm.
And some can be totally different!

It takes a special combination of ingredients
to make a good cake.

It takes a special combination of ingredients to make a family, too.

Each family has its own ingredients, its own kind of love
and its own rules — which is why every family is different.

Families can share the tough times,
help you learn from mistakes,
and encourage you when you might
feel a little bit flat.

Families also help celebrate wonderful moments
and give you the careful opportunities to do the things
you might never do with others.

It takes all kinds of different ingredients to make a cake.

And it can take many different ingredients to make a family, too.

Families have people, traditions, games and stories that hold them together.

They have rules and they have laughter.

Sometimes the ingredients are the same and sometimes we mix it up a little bit.

Sometimes a family might share a name and sometimes people with different names can make up a wonderful family.

There is no right or wrong type of cake, and there is no right or wrong type of family.

It doesn't really matter where the family is,
where they live, or how big they are, but when they
work together they are oh so good!

You are a very important part of your family mix.
You might even belong in different ways
to different parts of your family.

When we are making a delicious cake, it's important that we give it the right support it needs until it is quite ready.

Without support, things can get a bit messy.

While we are growing, we need help and support from others.
Our families keep a watchful eye on us.

They set limits and tell us what to do
so that we can stay safe and
turn out to be amazing.

It doesn't really matter how the support looks,
as long as it is the right kind of support for us.

A family's love, traditions, rules and laughter can
hold the family together – even if things get wobbly.

Cakes don't always turn out the way that we hope.

Some families might need some extra help to try to get things to turn out.

As we get older, families mean different things to us.
We might start thinking about forming our own part of the family...

adding a special other person, choosing our own mix and
making a whole new family batch.

Everyone has different ideas about what
type of cake is the best.

The best kind of family cake is the one that has loving ingredients,
kind support, and some help if things get too sticky.

Families can be the making of us.
Families can be the treat you have every day.

Yum.
Delicious!